Secrets of a Leadership Coach Guidebook

By Marshall Goldsmith, Bruce Gordon, Chris Coffey,
and Daniel Farb

Please send any correspondence regarding permissions to:
UniversityOfHealthCare
419 N. Larchmont Blvd., #323
Los Angeles, CA 90004

Secrets of a Leadership Coach Guidebook

ISBN: 1594912351

Library of Congress Catalog Number: 2005923179

UniversityOfHealthCare website: www.uohc.com

Neither the author nor the publisher assumes any liability for the information contained in this title. Every reader is responsible to determine his own situation and employ the techniques in this manual to the specific situation.

Contents

Introduction

This book is a text-only version of the CD products on sales humor writing and delivery skills. We have made it for those who prefer books. However, we have tried to retain the flavor of the CD approach.

You can find review questions scattered throughout the book. Cases and examples taken from the CD are included.

Although we usually mention sales situations throughout the book, we mean to include most business situations as well.

About the Authors

M. DANIEL FARB, CEO of UniversityOfHealthCare and UniversityOfBusiness, is a leader in the field of interactive management and healthcare e-learning. He received a BA in English Literature from Yale (where he set an academic record and studied with writers like Robert Penn Warren), an M.D. from Boston University, a degree in Executive Management from the Anderson School of Business at UCLA, and is currently working on a degree at UCLA in International Trade. He is a practicing ophthalmologist. He also has received two patents in ophthalmology and is working on others, has worked with the World Health Organization in Geneva and the National Institutes of Health in Washington, D.C. He has written scientific and popular articles, and has worked as a newspaper reporter. He helped Dr. Robbins edit one of the editions of Robbins' "Pathology" textbook for readability. He wrote an article on humor for the Massachusetts Review. He has experience in theater and television, including acting, directing, and stage-managing. He has programmed his own patient records database. He has written and edited hundreds of e-learning courses.

Dr. Farb is a member of the American Academy of Ophthalmology, the Union of American Physicians and Dentists, the AOJS, the American Association of Physicians and Surgeons, the ASTD (American Society for Training and Development), the E-Learning Forum, the Southern California Biomedical Council, the PDA (Parenteral Drug Association), and the Medical Marketing Association.

BRUCE GORDON is the Creative Director for UniversityOfHealthCare. After receiving a BA in Economics from UCLA, he began a freelance writing career that included technical writing (such as a manual for Princess Cruise Lines), stand-up comedy routines for nationally known comedians, and screenplay writing. He has done production support work with famous Hollywood personalities on such well-known productions as Aaron Spelling's "Dynasty" and "Love Boat" TV shows. An audio-visual software specialist, he is a versatile artist, with published works in a variety of media, including music, motion graphics, and digital video short film.

MARSHALL GOLDSMITH is one of the world's foremost authorities in helping leaders achieve positive, measurable change in behavior: for themselves, their people, and their teams. Marshall has been ranked in the Wall Street Journal as one of the "Top 10" consultants in the field of executive development. His work has received national recognition from the Institute for Management Studies, the American Management Association, the American Society for Training and Development and the Human Resource Planning Society. His coaching process has been positively described in both the New York Times and the Financial Times. Marshall is a managing partner of A4SL, the Alliance for Strategic Leadership, a consulting organization that includes over 100 top consultants in the field of leadership development. He is also the co-founder of the Financial Times Knowledge Dialogue, a videoconference network that connects executives with thought leaders. The FTKD enables his clients to discuss their unique issues with the world's greatest thinkers. He has a Ph.D. from UCLA. He is on the faculty of the global executive education program for Dartmouth and Oxford (UK) Universities. Marshall is a partner with Duke Corporate Education in the development of their personal learning practice. He is a member of the Board of the Peter Drucker Foundation. Marshall is one of a select few consultants who has been asked to work with over 50 major CEOs. His clients have included corporations, such as: 3M, Accenture, American Express, AHP, Aventis, Boeing, CalPERS, Chase Bank, GE, General Mills, Glaxo SmithKline, IBM, Johnson & Johnson, KPMG, McKinsey, Motorola, Pitney Bowes, Southern Company, Sun Microsystems, Thomson, UBS, and Weyerhaeuser. He has helped to implement leadership development processes that have impacted over one million people. Aside from his corporate work, Marshall has completed substantial volunteer projects for organizations such as: the Urban League; Save the Children; the Institute for East West Studies; the Girl Scouts; and the International, Canadian and American Red Cross (where he was a "National Volunteer of the Year"). Marshall's twelve recent books include: The Leader of the Future (a Business Week "Top 15" best-seller), Learning Journeys and Coaching for Leadership. The Leadership Investment won the American Library Association's Choice award as an "Outstanding Academic Business Book" of 2001. Amazon.com has ranked five of his books as the #1 best sellers in their field.

CHRIS COFFEY received a B.S. degree in marketing and a minor in philosophy. After graduation, he signed on with the U.S. Navy. After many years acting and directing, he began to do business consulting in 1984 and led "The Excellent Manager Workshop" for middle managers and above at IBM, Warner Lambert, Citibank, Apple and many other fortune 500 companies. Twice a year he teaches in the UCLA Technical Manager program, where he teaches scientists from government labs: Lawrence Livermore, Sandia, and Los Alamos. He has taught management and leadership at Gonzaga University in Florence, Italy. He is a member of the Alliance for Strategic Leadership.

Secrets of a Leadership Coach 1 Executive Coaching Techniques

With his "Coaching and Feedback" development process, most of Marshall Goldsmith's work has been focused on changing leadership behavior. This is his profession. However, these techniques are applicable to changing almost any interpersonal behavior. The process can help you—and the people around you—become better team members, suppliers, partners, spouses, or parents.

By becoming aware of how we can improve, involving people that we respect, and following up, we can almost always get better at the most important behavior as perceived by the most important people.

Your challenge in changing behavior will not be in <u>understanding</u> the process described in the series. Your challenge will be in <u>applying</u> this process in your day-to-day interactions. The techniques are designed to maximize your probabilities of actually <u>using</u> the material to help you and the people around you have more successful and happier lives.

In almost all cases, even the most successful leaders can increase their effectiveness by changing certain elements of their behavior. (The same is true for us as spouses, partners, friends, parents, or children.)

It has also been found that the key beliefs that help us succeed can become challenges when it is time for us to change. In many ways it can be harder for successful people to change.

What Leadership Is

People often ask about leadership. They want to know the qualities of a leader and they ask what it takes to be a leader.

They usually get the answer, "A leader needs to have a vision."

If you have a vision, you need to be able to communicate that vision in a way that other people understand it and understand the importance to them, so that they're willing to follow.

One of the purposes of this course is to teach how to develop leaders by executive coaching. The following thoughts show us where people will help a leader if a leader truly understands his role.

What's the role of a leader?
A leader's role is to raise other people's aspirations for what they can become and to get them to release their energies so that they will try. It's not the role of the leader to do everything.

Yet you cannot be a leader unless people are willing to follow your example of what it is you do.

What you say is important… what you do is more important.

Review Question: All a leader has to do to be successful is to have a vision. People will automatically understand and follow it. True or false?
Answer: False. If you as a leader have a vision, you need to be able to communicate that vision in a way that other people get it, understand it, and understand the importance to them, so that they're willing to follow.

Other qualities of a leader are:

* Inner-driven
* Other-focused
* Looking out for the good of other people

A person doesn't have to be a behavioral scientist to sense when somebody wants to lead for his own self-aggrandizement—vs. for the betterment of the people who are willing to follow.

What's in it for <u>them</u> if you become better at delegating?

If they see it only as them getting more work piled on their plate so that you can play golf, that's probably not going to be a motivating force for them. But it's a different story, however, if they're looking for you to delegate more effectively so that they can truly reach their potential—to where <u>they</u> want to go. Now, that will become a motivator for them. The best leaders understand what motivates other people. The mistake we often make in attempting to be leaders is that we make the assumption that what motivates us motivates others.

The key here is how you involve others in your improvement.

++++The Goldsmith technique involves others in that improvement.

<u>Behaviors to Change</u>

Learning what to avoid can be just important as learning what to do. Not enough time is spent teaching successful people what to stop. Half of the leaders that Marshall and his associates have met don't need to learn what to do. They need to learn what to stop!

What are some typical behaviors that need improvement?

Most of the successful people Marshall works with are incredibly bright and, often, this high IQ comes with some dysfunctional behaviors. Some common issues with successful people are the following:
* Impatience
* Not letting other people finish a sentence
* Figuring out what other people have to say before they say it
* Trying to be right too much.
* Not treating people with enough respect
* Coming across to people as arrogant or opinionated

Another common issue is that successful people try to win too much. If it is important, we try to win, if it is meaningful we try to win, if it is trivial we try to win, and if it is not worth it, we try to win anyway.

Case Study Illustration (Of Winning Too Much):

Assume that you want to go out to dinner at Restaurant X, your significant other wants to go to Restaurant Y and you have an argument. You end up going to Restaurant Y. The food is terrible and the service is awful.

You have two options:

Option A: Critique the food and service, demonstrate that your significant other was wrong, and that this debacle could have been avoided if only the person had listened to the ever so wise "me"!

Option B: Be quiet, eat the food, try to enjoy it, and have a nice evening.

Seventy percent of the successful people usually fail this test (according to their own definition of "failure"), they choose Option A and say they should have chosen Option B. This is a common issue that a leadership coach deals with.

If we do a "cost-benefit analysis" we usually realize that our relationship with our partner is far more important than winning a trivial argument about the quality of the food at dinner.

It's better to let the other people be right, and quit winning small points. Marshall often helps successful people focus on "winning the big ones" and "letting go of the little ones."

The next time you find yourself needing to "win" an argument, take a deep breath and ask yourself a simple question, "Is it worth it?"

People who are highly driven to succeed often experience something called "goal obsession"--which means that they become so obsessed with achieving goals that they engage in behavior that is inconsistent with the larger mission.

There is a huge gap between "I know the theory" and "I have changed my behavior." One of the greatest mistakes in all of leadership development is the assumption that "If we understand, we will do." There is little research to support this assumption.

Most of us understand that if we go on a healthy diet and work out every day we will be in better shape. We believe that this is the right thing for us to do. We just don't do it! Almost all of the leaders that Marshall meets are incredibly bright. Getting them to understand is easy. Getting them to do is a much greater challenge. This is true for all of us.

Successful executives need to learn from the people around them. These people are stakeholders in that executive's progress.

Who are the key stakeholders around the person being coached?
* All the direct reports
* A subset of colleagues
* Anybody at a higher level who has a direct impact on this person's success
Answering a question like this will help one determine the key stakeholders: "Who are the 8 to 10 people around you that will know if you've delegated more effectively?"

We need to find out how the key stakeholders view the person relative to those key behaviors. ~look at Hay material~

~MID YEAR REVIEW PROCESS~ **In this process it is very important to agree "up front" on (1) the desired behaviors and (2) the key stakeholders – otherwise successful people may say the process involved the wrong behavior or the feedback came from the wrong people. Marshall spends quite a bit of time getting buy-in before the process begins.**

It is also very important for the person being coached to understand that the behavior we are trying to change is the most important behavior for high leverage impact. It is not just some randomly picked low scoring behavior.

Executives being coached should not just say, "I guess I should get better at that." How should leaders choose the correct behaviors to change? They have to answer the question, "If I get better at this key behavior, is it going to make a real difference for me and the company?"

The following commitments are necessary before starting:
* Committing to getting feedback.
* Committing to, and publicly identify, the behaviors to work on.
* Committing to having one-on-one dialogues with all of the people who are significant stakeholders.
* Apologizing for previous mistakes.
* Saying he or she is not going to make excuses for his previous behavior.
* Following up on a regular basis
* Getting re-measured

If the person doesn't want to do those things, Marshall says: "That is fine, but I won't work with you."

The leader needs to say the following--or something very similar--to each stakeholder to fulfill the first part of the steps just mentioned:
"I am going through this coaching process and I just got some feedback. I really appreciate participating in a process like this. I appreciate the time and the energy you have taken to give me good feedback. The issues you gave feedback on are very meaningful to me. There are a couple of things I would like to improve.

"One is that I want to do a better job of treating people with respect.

"Also, I may have come across to some people as arrogant or opinionated in the past. If I have ever done that around you

please accept my apologies. There is no excuse for this behavior, but I cannot change the past.

"If you have a couple of ideas to help me do a better job of treating people with respect in the future, what would they be?"

Common example: Feedback from stakeholders might come back that an executive is micromanaging and has his fingers in everything. If the executive says that he needs to work on delegating, then he's asking for skill development. That's different from acknowledging that he is opinionate and needs to listen to others. That's a behavior that takes effort to change. Changing the behavior of not listening will lead to the development of better delegation skills.

Review Question: Which of the following is true about the process?
a) Behavioral change is measured by the selected significant stakeholders.
b) Behavioral change is measured by the coach.
c) Behavioral change is measured by the leader.
Answer: a.

Feedforward

The process utilizes a type of feedback process known as "feedforward." A way of asking for feedforward was demonstrated in the previous paragraph. Feedforward occurs when a person is asked to listen to suggestions for the future and *learn as much as he or she can.* Feedforward also happens when a person gives someone else suggestions for the future and *helps as much as he or she can.* ***Both speaker and listener can participate in feedforward!

Traditional feedback focuses on a *past* - that cannot be changed - not a *future* that can be changed. In this sense, feedback can be limited and static, as opposed to the expansive and dynamic nature of feedforward.

One of the keys to the success of the feedforward process is that it focuses on the future, not the past. "Letting go" of the past is easy in theory. It can be difficult in practice.

Many of us have not forgiven our mothers and fathers for not being the "perfect parents" that we thought they should have been. We haven't forgiven our children for not being the "ideal children" or our partners for not being the "dream partner" that they were supposed to be.

At work, holding on to the past can be just as obvious. Employees are often "punished" for comments they made have made years ago. Managers are not forgiven for lacking foresight to see what looked obvious after the fact.

Cognitive dissonance theory is one of the best-researched theories in psychology. We all tend to view people in a manner that is consistent with our previously existing stereotype. We look for behavior that reinforces this stereotype. The closer we are to people, the more this is the case.

The *last* person who believes that we are going to change is often our spouse, significant other, or partner. If you don't think that this is true, leave this program and announce to your partner that you are taking a new course on changing behavior and that you are going to become a better partner in the relationship. Watch your partner's face. The most common reaction is laughter!

The feedforward process has produced such a positive reaction that it has become the base of all of Marshall's work in behavioral coaching. The key is focusing on the future.

Why feedforward works for changing behavior

- While successful people often don't like disconfirming feedback, they love getting ideas for the future. We greatly appreciate ideas that are aimed at helping us change behavior that *we* have defined as important. We are more than willing to try to improve in areas that we have defined as needing improvement. Successful people tend to have a high need for self-determination and will tend to accept ideas about concerns that they "own" while rejecting ideas that feel "forced" upon them. Many successful executives enjoy getting feedforward. Negative feedback seldom produces this type of positive reaction.

- *We can change the future. We can't change the past.* Feedforward helps people envision and focus on a positive future, not a failed past. Athletes are often trained using feedforward. Racecar drivers are taught to, "look at the road, not the wall." Basketball players are taught to envision the ball going in the hoop and to imagine the perfect shot. By giving people ideas on how they can be even more successful, we can increase their chances of achieving this success in the future.

- *It can be more productive to help people be "right," than prove they were "wrong."* As we discussed earlier, negative feedback often becomes an exercise in "let me prove you were wrong." This tends to produce defensiveness on the part of the receiver and discomfort on the part of the sender. Even constructively delivered feedback is often seen as negative as it necessarily involves a discussion of mistakes, shortfalls, and problems. Feedforward, on the other hand, is almost always seen as positive because it focuses on *solutions* not *problems*.

- *People do not take feedforward as personally as feedback.* As we discussed, it is virtually impossible to give a successful person negative behavioral feedback and have them not "take it personally". Feedforward is not seen as an insult or "put down". It is hard to get offended about a suggestion aimed at helping us get better at what we want to improve (especially if we are not forced to implement the suggestion).

- *Feedback can reinforce personal stereotyping and negative self-fulfilling prophecies.* Feedforward can reinforce the possibility of change. Feedback can reinforce the feeling of failure. How many of us have been "helped" by a spouse, significant other or friend, who seems to have a near-photographic memory of our previous "sins" that they share with us in order to point out the history of our shortcomings. Negative feedback can be used to reinforce the message, "this is just the way you are". Feedforward is based on the assumption that we can make positive changes in the future.

- *Face it! Most of us hate getting negative feedback!* Marshall says,
I have reviewed summary 360° feedback reports for over 50 companies. The item, "encourages and accepts constructive criticism" almost always scores near the bottom on co-worker satisfaction with leaders. Although it is "politically correct" to pretend to like negative feedback, most of us find it to be awful. The fact that most leaders are not skilled at giving negative feedback only makes it worse!

- *When receiving feedforward the "listener" can focus on* hearing *without having to worry about* responding. One participant in the exercise made a very profound observation. He said, "This was great because I didn't have to worry about composing my clever response while the other person was talking! All I could say was 'Thank you.' Most of the time I don't listen that well because I am so focused on my response that I miss part of what the other person is saying."

- *Feedforward makes us listen patiently and not interrupt.* Higher-ranking members of organizations are more likely to interrupt others than lower-level members. Impatience when listening is one of the most common problems of smart, successful people. Practicing feedforward makes us "shut up and listen" while others are speaking.

Why feedforward works for the sender of suggestions

- *People love to give helpful suggestions when asked.* Participants in this exercise not only appreciate getting suggestions, they also enjoy *giving* suggestions. The key is "when asked". If others ask for our input, listen and thank us – we feel great! Most people like to help others. However, it usually seems rude or intrusive to try to "help" someone who has not asked for out assistance.

- *The sender receives thanks for positive suggestions, not punishment for negative feedback.* While negative feedback often produces a negative or even punishing response, feedforward only results in thanks. This is hard not to like!

- *We don't have to "prove" that our suggestions are good ideas.* In the feedforward process, our ideas are not judged. If the receiver likes the suggestion, he or she may use it. If not, it can just be ignored. This eliminates fear and defensiveness on the part of the sender.

- *We don't have to be an expert on the topic.* The feedforward process is designed to provide ideas about interpersonal behavior. Almost anyone in an organization knows what this means. You don't have to be an "expert" on listening to know what good listening means to you. A common misconception of coaching is that we have to be an expert to help someone else. In many cases we are better off not being an expert, but just being a fellow human being!

- *We don't have to be an expert on the person.* Another misconception about coaching is that someone has to have a "deep understanding" of us in order to help us. This is far from true. Participants in this exercise frequently comment about how much they can learn from people that they have never met.

- *Face it! Most of us hate giving negative feedback.* In our review of 360° feedback summaries, the item "provides developmental feedback in a timely manner" is another one that almost always scores near the bottom in terms of employee's satisfaction with their managers. Training in this area doesn't seem to help much. If leaders got better at providing negative feedback every time the performance appraisal process was changed, they would all be perfect by now!

- *Feedforward can cover almost all of the same "material" as feedback.* Imagine that you have just made a terrible presentation in front of the executive committee. Your manager is in the room. Rather than make you "relive" this humiliating experience, your manager might help you prepare for future presentations by giving you suggestions for the future. These suggestions can be very specific and still delivered in a positive way. In this way your manager can "cover the same points" without feeling as embarrassed and without making you feel even more humiliated.

- *Feedforward can be a useful tool to apply with managers, peers and team members.* Rightly or wrongly, feedback is associated with judgment. This can lead to very negative unintended consequences when applied to managers or peers. Feedforward does not imply superiority of judgment. It is more focused on being a helpful "fellow traveler" than an "expert". As such it can be easier to hear from a person who is not in a position of power or authority. An excellent team building exercise is to have each team member ask, "How can I better help our team in the future?" and listen to feedforward from fellow team members (in one-on-one dialogues.)

Why feedforward works for both parties

- *Feedforward tends to be much faster and more efficient than feedback.* An excellent technique for giving ideas to successful people is to say, "Here are four ideas for the future. Please accept these in the positive spirit that they are given. If you can only use two of the ideas, you are still two ahead. Just ignore what doesn't make sense for you." With this approach almost no time gets wasted on judging the quality of the ideas or "proving that the ideas are wrong." This "debate" time is usually negative; it can take up a lot of time, and it is often not very productive. By eliminating

- 18 -

judgment of the ideas, the process becomes much more efficient for the sender, as well as the receiver.

- *Both parties are both giving and listening to suggestions.* This two-way quality of the exercise feels like "two colleagues helping each other" not "a superior being providing a critique".

- *When we help the other person, we help ourselves.* One of the most common comments made during the feedforward exercise is, "I have that problem, too!" We all like to think that we are unique and that our issue and concerns are unusual. In most cases, both parties could benefit from improving at the behavior that either is discussing. Another common reaction is, "I should listen to my own suggestions!" The suggestions that we give others are often ideas that we need to implement in our own lives.

Feedforward is not feedback. This course is not written with the intent to show that feedback is always bad or dysfunctional. Feedback can be very useful for understanding where "were we are" in terms of either results or behavior.

Obviously, sales people need feedback on what is selling and what isn't. Leaders need feedback on how they are perceived by their colleagues.

As far as the usefulness of negative feedback goes, research on performance appraisals generally shows that the appraisal meeting is *not* a useful time for coaching.

Performance appraisals almost always involve a *judgment.* This is not necessarily bad. This is just what an "appraisal" is.

Studies show that when people are being "judged" they tend to focus on the accuracy of the rating or judgment, not on how they can improve.

*****Marshall's suggestion for managers is not to avoid negative feedback. It is to separate feedback about the past from coaching for the future.**

* Give people time to think about feedback without having to react.

* Reach an agreement on whatever judgment is needed and then "move on" toward the future.

* Try not to stereotype people based on a previous mistake.

If the person has a behavioral issue, try to get an agreement on what the issue is. The more that people agree with the behavioral assessment, the more likely they are to try to change.

If people are willing to try to change, then the feedforward coaching process will almost always help. If they don't care, you have three options:
*1) Fire them (if their behavior is a violation of your organization's values and they don't want to change – this can be the best plan).
*2) Put them on some kind of "probation" (which seldom works).
*3) "Let it go" (if the behavior is not very important this may be the best plan).

360 degree feedback means getting feedback from all of the people around you. So, 360 would represent the person above you (for example, your manager), to the side of you, (peers and

colleagues), and the people below you on the organizational chart (your direct reports).

There is some confusion about this. People often think that anytime you get feedback, it's 360 feedback. But it's not really 360 unless it includes all of the people mentioned above that work around you, with you in the middle.

Sometimes you do feedback where it would just involve the manager, with his or her direct reports. You often hear of that referred to as 180 feedback. Another term used is 270 feedback, which would include peers and direct reports.

This is what Marshall says about 360 degree feedback:
I still believe that confidential 360° feedback can be a very useful process. I am less convinced about the value of non-confidential 360° feedback – if the goal is individual development. Several studies have indicated the confidential feedback is both more accurate and more useful for developmental purposes. Even Jack Welch, who was once a staunch proponent of 360° feedback for evaluation has concluded that this can "politicize" the process so that it becomes almost useless in a few years.

In my work as a coach, I often use 360° feedback to help people establish a base for "where they are." I then move to feedforward to help people get to "where they want to be."

Review Question: Which of the following is the INCORRECT statement for a leader to make to key stakeholders when asking for feedback?
A) "I've made mistakes in the past before. I'm only human. I bet you've made mistakes, too, haven't you?"
B) "I'm sorry for any mistakes I've made in the past."

C) "I'm not going to make any excuses for my previous behavior."
Answer: A.

Challenges to Changing

Everything being taught here is specifically designed to deal with the specifics of leading successful people and helping successful people change. There are, however, some key challenges in this process of helping successful people change. Almost every person that Marshall works with has the potential to be a good, if not great, manager of people. He believes that many more people have the potential for leadership than most of us recognize.

Many potentially good leaders are "written off" because they have interpersonal difficulties. Most research in the field indicates the interpersonal issues are the major cause of "derailment" for high-potential leaders. Many people achieve great success in operational assignments and then "crash" when they are given managerial responsibilities. They often assume the behavior that led to their technical success will also work when they become managers.

Successful people can be coached to become even more successful by helping them to change their behavior. But this is no easy feat, since successful people didn't get where they are by being humble.

Successful people tend to have a few basic beliefs, each of which makes it hard to change.
* I choose to succeed.
* I can succeed.
* I will succeed.

* I have succeeded.

Each of these beliefs increases our likelihood of achieving success but can make it hard for us to change. Successful people are very committed. That's normally a good thing, but they get so committed it's hard for them to realize sometimes that their strategy is the wrong strategy and they're headed in the wrong direction.

Review Question: Why do many who people achieve great success in operational assignments "crash" when they are given managerial responsibilities?
Answer: They often assume (incorrectly) that the behavior that led to their technical success will also work when they become managers.

Successful people's personal commitment and ownership can make it hard for them to change.

Successful people have a phenomenal need for something called "self-determination." If you try to make them change, you are unlikely to succeed! The change needs to come from them.

Belief number 1: "I choose to succeed." Successful people believe that they are doing what they choose to do, because they choose to do it.

Successful people are very committed. That's normally a good thing, but they get so committed it's hard for them to realize sometimes that their strategy is the wrong strategy and they're headed in the wrong direction.

"I choose to succeed" is a belief that is highly correlated with achievement in virtually any field. Adding "and I choose to change" can be a very difficult transition.

Successful people have a high need for self-determination. The more successful a person is, the more likely this is to be true. When we do what we *choose* to do, we are *committed*. When we do what we *have* to do, we are *compliant*. It is easy to observe the impact of this type of commitment in jobs where money is not related to performance. For example, high-school teachers who are teaching because they have a "calling" for the profession of teaching clearly stand out from teachers who are teaching because they feel they have to be doing it to make a living.

Having the belief, "I choose to succeed" does not imply that successful people are selfish. Obviously, many successful people are great team players. It does mean that successful people need to feel a *personal* commitment to what they are doing. They need a sense of ownership. When leaders have a personal commitment to the mission, they will be much more likely to achieve results. They will lead with their hearts as well as their minds. They will also be effective in attracting and developing fellow "believers" who want to get the job done.

Marshall's attitude is as follows:

Successful people have a unique distaste for feeling controlled or manipulated. In my work, I have "made peace" with the fact that I cannot "make" successful leaders change. I can only help them get better at what they choose to change. One of the great challenges of coaching (or teaching or parenting) is to realize that the ultimate motivation for change has to come from the person being coached, not the coach.

The more we believe that our behavior is a result of our own choices and commitments, the less likely we are to want to change our behavior. The underlying theory (cognitive dissonance) is simple. The more we are committed to believing that something is true, the less likely we are to be willing to change our beliefs (even in the face of clear evidence that shows we are wrong).

Review Question: What is the theory behind the psychological principle called cognitive dissonance?
a) The less we are committed to believing that something is true, the less likely we are to be willing to change our beliefs (even in the face of clear evidence that shows we are wrong).
b) The more we are committed to believing that something is true, the less likely we are to be willing to change our beliefs (even in the face of clear evidence that shows we are wrong).
Answer: b.

Belief number 2: Successful people believe: "I can succeed." (That is generally positive, but they tend to over-commit.)

That's why it's very important to help them focus on that one key issue, and not let them talk with you about 20 things that are going to change.

Successful people believe that they have the internal capacity to make desirable things happen. This is the definition of self-efficacy. Self-efficacy is perhaps the most central belief shown to drive individual success. People who believe they can succeed see opportunities where others see threats.

This comfort with ambiguity leads people with high self-efficacy to take greater risks and achieve greater returns. To put it simply, they try more different things!

Successful people tend to have a high "internal locus of control." In other words, they do not feel like victims of fate. They believe that they have the motivation and ability to change their world.

They see success for themselves and others as largely a function of people's motivation and ability - not luck, random chance or external factors. Successful people want to "bet" on themselves and the people that they trust!

While the "I can succeed" belief is generally associated with success, it can (when combined with optimism) lead to what is called "superstitious behavior." This "superstition" can lead to difficulty in changing behavior even when others see this behavior as obviously flawed.

Here is an example of the "I can succeed" challenge from Marshall's own experiences.
"A few years ago, I was able to make a lot of money due to factors that were almost totally outside of my control. To put it simply, I was just lucky!

When describing this event to my friends almost all said that my good fortune had little to do with luck. It was really a function of my hard work. While I do work very hard, my hard work had nothing to do with this success.

This is a classic response from successful people. My friends tended to believe that success is "earned" through an individual's motivation and ability (even when it is not)."

We have now discussed two surprising reasons that can make it hard for successful people to change. Successful people tend to be both delusional and superstitious!

Successful people often confuse correlation with causality. This is the mathematical definition of "superstition". They often do not realize that they are successful "because of" some behaviors and "in spite of" others. Any human (in fact, any animal) will tend to repeat behavior that is followed by positive reinforcement. The more successful people become, the more positive reinforcement they tend to receive. One of the greatest mistakes of successful people is the assumption, "I am successful. I behave this way. Therefore, I must be successful *because* I behave this way!" "Superstitious behavior" is merely the confusion of correlation and causality. Many leaders get positive reinforcement for the *results* that occur. They then assume that their behavior is what helped lead to these results.

Just as successful athletes believe in "lucky" numbers or perform "rituals" before a contest, successful business leaders tend to repeat behaviors that are followed by rewards. They may fear that changing *any* behavior will break their "string of success".

Successful people face the real danger of confusing "because of" and "in spite of" when analyzing why they are successful. (In other words, success "because of" one's behavior versus success "in spite of" one's behavior.)

One financial services CEO was viewed as an outstanding leader, but was seen as incredibly weak in the area of providing coaching to his direct reports. (This is fairly common for top executives.)

He had developed an elaborate rationalization as to:
1) Why coaching "at my level" was not important
2) Why coaching was a waste of his time
3) How he had "made it this far" without providing coaching
4) How *he* had never received much coaching and it obviously did not hurt *his* career!

Fortunately, this executive had some highly respected direct reports who were both courageous and assertive. He decided to honor their wishes and give coaching a try.

After undergoing successful coaching, he finally admitted that this had been a personal weakness for years. He realized he had been successful in spite of his lack of coaching, not because of it.

The next time you have a great success – stop and ask yourself a hard question, "What was probably on my 'in spite of' list?"

When looking to the future, you should realize that yesterday's "because of" can become tomorrow's "in spite of".

I Can Succeed: Confusing "Because Of and "In Spite Of"

A macro-level example of this phenomenon has occurred in Japan. In the 1980s, Japanese managers were widely praised as role models for leadership behavior. The country's economic growth was one of the greatest "success stories" in the history of business. Books were written and "benchmarking trips" were organized so that leaders from around the world could learn from their success. This success had a deep impact on many leaders. Business success went beyond financial results and was transformed into national pride about "Japanese management." Leaders were not just proud of what they had achieved, they were proud of how they achieved it.

Unfortunately, the style that worked in the 1980s did not work in the 1990s. Rapid changes in technology, the economy, the role of manufacturing and the workforce made the "Japanese management" approach far less desirable. It has taken a decade for many leaders in Japan to admit that their previous approach was no longer working. Many leaders "denied the numbers" for years, before accepting the fact that change was needed. The same management style that had brought a huge success in the 1980s, led to a huge challenge by the turn of the century. The leaders who have had the wisdom and courage to "let go" of the past are the ones who are succeeding in the new Japanese economy.

Belief number 3: "I will succeed."

An unflappable sense of optimism is one of the most important characteristics of successful people.

Successful people not only believe that they *can* achieve, they believe that they *will* achieve. This belief goes beyond any one task. Successful leaders tend to communicate with an overall sense of self-confidence.

Successful people tend to pursue opportunities. If they set a goal, write the goal down, and publicly announce the goal, they will tend to do "whatever it takes" to achieve the goal.

Successful people tend to pursue opportunities. If they set a goal, write the goal down, and publicly announce the goal, they will tend to do "whatever it takes" to achieve the goal. Successful people tend to be extremely busy and face the danger of over-commitment. When they don't implement the behavioral plan they start, they usually say, "I was over-committed and just did not get to it!"

While this sense of optimism is generally associated with success, it can easily lead to "overload" if it is not controlled.

The Danger of Over-Commitment

In a recent study with Accenture involving over 200 high-potential leaders (from 120 companies around the world), self-confidence ranked as one of the "top 10" elements of effective leadership for leaders in the past, the present and the future.

Successful leaders not only believe that they will achieve, they assume that the people they respect will achieve. As was stated earlier, they see success as a function of people's motivation and ability. If they believe that their people have the motivation and ability, they communicate this contagious sense of belief, optimism and self-confidence to others. This leads to increased motivation, increased performance and increased success.

Successful people tend to be extremely busy and face the danger of over-commitment.

Marshall observes the following:

It can be difficult for an ambitious person, with an "I will succeed attitude," to say "no" to desirable opportunities. As of this writing, the huge majority of executives that I work with feel as busy (or busier) today than they have ever felt in their lives. In North America, this perception was consistent for the last four years of the '90s, a decade which featured one of the longest economic expansions in our history. Most of these executives were not over-committed because they were trying to "save a sinking ship." They were over-committed because they were "drowning in a sea of opportunity." A recent Harris poll has shown that the biggest "stressor" for high-income people (by a factor of 50%) is "too many things to do."

While successful people achieve a lot, they often believe that they can do more than they can. My favorite European "volunteer" client was the Executive Director of one of the world's leading human services organizations. His mission was to help the world's most vulnerable people. Unfortunately (for all of us), his business was booming. His biggest challenge as a leader, by far, was avoiding over-commitment. (By the way, this is very common for the top human services leaders.) Without externally imposed discipline, he had a tendency to promise even more than the most dedicated staff could deliver. Unchecked, this "we will succeed" attitude could lead to staff "burn out," high turnover, and ultimately less capability to help those in need.

One of my clients recently completed a study of the graduates of their executive development program. As part of the program each graduate was expected to focus on behavioral change. They were all instructed in a simple process to help them achieve this change. At the end of the class almost 100% of the participants said that they would follow the steps in the process (in a confidential survey). One year later about 70% followed the process. This group showed huge improvement in effectively changing behavior. Approximately 30% did nothing. This group showed no more improvement than a control group.

When asked, "Why didn't you implement the behavioral change plan that you said you would?" "I was over-committed and just did not get to it!" was by far the most common response.

Belief number 4: "I have succeeded."

Successful people tend to have a very positive interpretation of their past performance. High achievers not only believe that they have achieved results, they tend to believe that their contribution was key to the achievement of the results.

This tends to be true even if the positive outcomes were caused by factors that they did *not* control. In a positive way, successful people are "delusional". They tend to see their previous history as a validation of who they are and what they have done. While the belief, "I have succeeded" has many positive benefits, it can cause difficulty when behavioral change is needed.

In many successful partnerships, if you ask each partner to record the percent of his or her contribution to the profits of the partnership - the combined number is often 300%!

This (often unrealistically) positive interpretation of the past leads to increased optimism about the future and actually enhances their likelihood of future success. People with a positive self-image, who believe they have a history of success, tend to become more successful. This success reinforces the accuracy of our positive self-image and creates a "virtuous cycle" of positive reinforcement.

In no way does this "delusional" tendency imply that successful people tend to lack integrity. Most successful people have high amounts of personal integrity. We truly *believe* that we are better than we are!

While the belief, "I have succeeded" has many positive benefits; it can cause difficulty when behavioral change is needed. Successful people's positive view of their performance can make it hard for them to hear information to the contrary from others. Successful people consistently over-rate their performance relative to their professional peers.

We tend to accept feedback from others that is consistent with the way we see ourselves. We tend to reject or deny feedback from others that is inconsistent with the way we see ourselves. It can be very hard for successful people to hear that what they are doing is not effective.

The mini-survey, with its regular feedback, gives the coached leader the optimism and drive to succeed in his task of behavioral change.

Review Question: Which of the following is the correct attitude towards behavioral change?
A) "I became successful by doing things my way. I don't need to change anything."
B) "I was mulling over a few things I could change very easily. I think I should get better at those first."
C) "I'll choose a behavior to change only if doing so would make a real difference in the company."
Answer: C.

Leaders' Reaction to the Process

Leaders love this process because:
* It doesn't take much time
* It produces real, measurable results

It does not take much time because it is weaved into what one does anyway.

****Here's the key: Others determine the improvement.

Leaders love the process because it doesn't take endless time, and there is no risk.

Here is an example of what one coach says about the process: *Let's say we worked together and you picked two things you wanted to improve. I'd say, "Okay, who are the 8 or 10 people around you who would know if you improved at those things?" Twice through the course of the year, they will be sent a little mini-survey that will say: "Five months ago, Jake committed to do this.... On a scale of –3 to +3, has he improved?" So the improvement is not determined by me. It's not determined by you. It's determined by the people around you, who will be impacted.*

One coach said this about being hired as a personal consultant: "We as the consultants take a lot of the risk, because we don't get paid until a year after working with executives, and we only get paid if they improve. And we only get paid based on the level of improvement and the metrics that are put in place at the beginning of the process. Now another key thing about this is that we do not determine success."

The Goldsmith approach is: "How you engage the 8 or 10 people around this individual that are KEY to this individual's success?"

If this process works so well, why don't leaders always do this process?

It has nothing to do with ethics, integrity, values, or knowledge.

* It has to do with being busy.

And it has to do with a dream that many successful people have.

You know, I am incredibly busy right now. In fact, I feel about as busy today as I have ever felt. Some days I feel over-committed. In fact, every now and then my life feels out of control.

But we are working on some very unique and special challenges right now. I feel like the worst of this is going to be over in a couple or three months.

After that, I am going to take a couple of weeks, take a little time off, get organized, spend some time with the family and start working out. Everything is going to change. This time will be here soon. After that, it won't be crazy anymore!

Now, here is the reality:
* There is no "couple of weeks". Look at the trend line! Sanity does not prevail. There is a good chance that tomorrow is going to be just as crazy as today.
* If you want to change anything about yourself, when is the best time to start? Now! Ask yourself, "What am I willing to change now?" Just do that.

Marshall says that he is not ashamed of the fact that only 70% of the thousand leaders who went to his class did something. He's actually proud of that fact. Compared to most training and development, this number is outstanding!

Many of the people that learn this material will believe that they will do what is discussed and that they will achieve a positive, long-term change in behavior.

Many will do this. Some will not.

Marshall and his associates have interviewed hundreds of people that have participated in their training programs one year later. They asked the people who did nothing why they did not live up to the commitments that they made after they attended leadership training. As far as the CEO coaches can tell, most people who do nothing are no "worse" as human beings than the people who change. They are no less intelligent. They have about the same values.

Why don't they do what they committed to do?

It's because of the dream that was described earlier of waiting for that non-existent time period when they will no longer be busy.

How do you protect yourself against the "more time later" dream?
--Ask yourself: "What am I willing to change NOW?" And just work on it.
--When you coach people, ask them the challenge: "What are you willing to change NOW?" Have them just work on that.
--Don't waste your time dreaming about some fantasy world that's never really going to get here.
--Do what you can do today, make peace with it... and everything else... just take a deep breath....

...LET IT GO!

Summary:
* Figure out a profile of what you want to be.
* Get feedback on "Am I doing it?"
* Develop a plan that's positive, simple, and focused.

* Talk to people around you and involve them.
* Follow up (by giving a couple of mini-surveys) maybe once every six months.

If we follow the process, we almost always achieve a positive, measurable change in behavior.

Secrets of a Leadership Coach 2 Developing Ourselves as Leaders

Objectives

Upon the completion of this course, you will be able to...
1. List the 3 steps of encouraging feedback
2. Demonstrate how to thank people for their feedback
3. Write the 3 guidelines for responding to feedback
4. Describe how to involve other people in helping one change
5. Describe the follow-up process

In this course we will detail how a person can develop himself or herself as a leader. Before we can help other people change, the first person we have to help change is oneself.

To develop ourselves as leaders, we need to receive feedback from our key stakeholders concerning our behavior and develop ourselves first. Then you need to involve others in your improvement. We will address the above five objectives in order in this manual.

Encouraging Feedback

There are three general steps (memory aid: ALL) for encouraging feedback.

- Ask

- Listen
- Learn

Then there are other steps in developing ourselves.

Step 1: Ask for Feedback

Before you get started, do a 9-question self-assessment on how successful people get better to see where you stand in developing your leadership skills. Come back to this self-assessment in the future to see how you have changed.

1. How many times in the past month have you asked anyone for feedback on something you did?
___ **None**
___ **1-2 times**
___ **3-5 times**
___ **6-10 times**
___ **Over 10 times**

2. How many times in the past month have you asked anyone for suggestions on how to improve something?
___ **None**
___ **1-2 times**
___ **3-5 times**
___ **6-10 times**
___ **Over 10 times**

3. How often would others say you listen well?
___ **Never**
___ **Sometimes**
___ **Frequently**
___ **Most of the time**
___ **All of the time**

4. How frequently do you say "thank you" when others give you feedback or suggestions?
___ **Never**
___ **Sometimes**

__ Frequently
__ Most of the time
__ All of the time

5. How often do you think about the costs and benefits of your actions/behavior before acting?
__ Never
__ Sometimes
__ Frequently
__ Most of the time
__ All of the time

6. How often would others say you are defensive when you respond to their feedback or suggestions?
__ Never
__ Sometimes
__ Frequently
__ Most of the time
__ All of the time

7. How many people would you say they are actively involved in helping you improve as a leader and have been recognized for it?
__ No one
__ 1-2
__ 3-5
__ 6-10
__ Over 10

8. How effective have you been in changing your behavior as a leader?
__ Ineffective
__ Somewhat ineffective
__ Somewhat effective
__ Effective
__ Highly effective

9. To what extent would others describe you as following-up with them on your efforts to improve as a leader?

__ **Never**
__ **Sometimes**
__ **Frequently**
__ **Most of the time**
__ **All of the time**

Calculate your score by assigning 1 to the first answer, 2 to the second, 3 to the third, 4 to the fourth, 5 to the fifth, and adding up the numbers. The range can be 9-45.

Scores of 9 - 18 indicate a need to learn the above skills
Scores of 19 - 26 indicate the beginnings of the use of the above skills
Scores of 27 - 35 indicate a strong tendency to use the above skills
Scores of 36 - 45 indicate a competency in the above skills

The process of developing ourselves begins with asking key stakeholders (the 8-10 people most impacted by a person) for feedback. The person coached will have a one-on-one dialogue with each significant stakeholder to say something like the following:
* "I would like to do a better job of treating people with respect."
* "If I have come across as arrogant or opinionated in the past around you please accept my apologies. There is no excuse for this behavior, but I cannot change the past."
* "If you have a couple of ideas to help me do a better job of treating people with respect in the future, what would they be?"

Review Question: Which of the following is the INCORRECT response for a leader when the coach says:
"Before I work with you, you have to commit to and publicly identify the leadership behavior you want to improve."

A) "OK, I'll identify the behaviors I'll be working on publicly."
B) "I'll commit to behaviors I decide to work on."
C) "I'd feel more comfortable keeping my behavioral change work private, just like any medical or psychological therapy should be. If I decide to change my mind about working on something, that's just my business."
Answer: A

The most common behavioral problem of successful people is "winning too much."

An obsession with winning isn't just common in executives. It is common in most highly successful people – including Marshall (and his associates)!

When the issue is critical we want to win. When it is important we want to win. When it is trivial we want to win. When it is not worth it, we want to win anyway! Why? - Because we like to win.

An Example Of Winning Too Much

Gardiner Morse, in an interview that was published in the Harvard Business Review, asked Marshall to discuss the most common behavioral problem that he observed in the executives that he met. The answer was winning too much.

Here is an example that Marshall likes to use with his clients. Assume that you want to go to dinner at restaurant X. Your spouse, partner or friend wants to go to dinner at restaurant Y. You have a heated debate. You end up going to restaurant Y, which was not your choice. The food tastes like garbage and the service is awful. You have two options. Option A – Critique the food. Point out to your partner how wrong he or she was and how this debacle could have been avoided if you had been listened to. Option B – Shut up! Eat the food. Try to enjoy it and have a nice evening.

What do 75% of Marshall's clients say they would do in this situation? Critique the food. What do they agree that they should do? Shut up and have a good time!

In Marshall's volunteer work with the United States Army, he teaches a leadership class for Generals. He always uses this dinner case study. The Generals have a huge disadvantage when they work with Marshall. Their spouse comes to the program with them! It is very hard to deny what you would do in a situation involving your spouse, when your spouse is staring at you while you are talking. Even the wisest of Generals can find it challenging to "shut up and enjoy dinner"!

If we do a "cost-benefit analysis" we usually realize that our relationship with our partner is far more important than winning a trivial argument about the quality of the food at dinner.

The next time you find yourself needing to "win" an argument, take a deep breath and ask yourself a simple question, "Is it worth it?"

What are some of the wrong responses we can give to a key stakeholder who has given us feedback we asked for regarding a behavior we want to improve?
* 1) We can tell people that they're confused
* 2) We can tell them they're a bunch of idiots

What is the correct response we should give to a key stakeholder who has given us feedback we asked for regarding a behavior we want to improve?
* We should say, "Thank you."

Another classic problem of successful people is punishing people who disagree with them.

How many times have you heard the following sermons preached in your organization?

- "We need to encourage people to express their opinions!"
- "We want people to challenge the system!"
- "We want to encourage those innovative and creative ideas!"
- "We want to *empower* people to tell us what they really think!"

These statements are heard a lot, but rarely realized.

An Example Of Punishing The Messenger

Marshall illustrates "punishing the messenger" from his personal life:

I will give you an example of a case when I totally "blew it" in the area of encouraging input from the most important person in my life. I will also predict that (when you read my example) you will agree that what I did was incredibly stupid. You may also admit that you have done exactly the same stupid thing that I did!

I fly almost every week. On American Airlines alone, I have over seven million frequent flyer miles. I always put off going to the airport until the last minute, so I am usually in a mad rush to get there. On this particular drive to the airport, my wife, Lynda, was sitting in the front seat. My two children, Kelly and Bryan were sitting in the back seat. As usual, I was late, driving too fast, and not paying attention. Lynda (who is, to make things worse, has a Ph. D. and a licensed clinical psychologist) said, "Look out! There's a red light up ahead!"

Being a trained behavioral science professional, a person that teaches others the value of encouraging input, what did I do? I screamed, "I know there's a red light! Don't you think I can see? I can drive as well as you can!"

When we arrived at the airport, did she kiss me goodbye? No. Did she speak to me? No. Was she upset with me? Yes!

During the long flight to New York, I did something that you have probably done many times before – a cost-benefit analysis. I asked myself, "What was the cost of her saying, 'There is a red light up ahead'?" No cost came to mind. "What was the potential benefit? What could have been saved?" Many benefits came to mind - my life, her life, the lives of our children and the lives of other innocent people that might have been saved.

When someone gives us something that has a huge potential benefit and costs absolutely nothing, what should we say to this fine person? "Thank you!"

I got off the plane in New York feeling guilty and ashamed. I called Lynda and told her my cost-benefit story. I said, "The next time that you help me with my driving, I am just going to say, 'Thank you.'" In her most sarcastic voice she replied, "Sure you will!" I said, "Just watch. I am going to do better!" "We'll see," she replied skeptically.

A few months passed, and I had long forgotten all about this incident. Again, I was racing to the airport, not paying attention, when Lynda said, "Look out for the stop sign!" My face turned red. I started breathing hard. I grimaced and then yelled, "Thank you!"

I am a long way from perfect, but I am getting better!

The next time someone "helps you" with your driving (or anything else important), try to remember this story and just say, "Thank you!"

ask
say
Thank you

How do you ask for feedback? Here is the basic formula:
"I want to be a better .... How can I ... better?"
Here is an example: "I want to be a better supplier. How can I serve you better?"
Then listen, take notes, and follow up. If we do this, their opinion of us as a supplier will go up.

Here are more examples:
"I want to be a better team player. How can I help the team?"
"I want to be a better manager. How can I better serve the staff?"

Step 2 - Listen to Feedback

When we ask for feedback, we set up an expectation in the minds of our stakeholders. The stakeholders will expect us to let them tell us what they think we need to do next.
They will expect that we will listen to what they have to say.

What is another wrong response we can give to a key stakeholder who has given us feedback we asked for regarding a behavior we want to improve? Ask for feedback, and then express our opinion.

Why shouldn't we express our opinion of the stakeholders' feedback?
Because when we do that, our opinion is likely to sound to the other person like...
* Defensiveness
* Denial
* Rationalization

* Making excuses

Step 3 (Thank) People for Feedback

When we get feedback, we should:
* Express gratitude
* Let people know how much we appreciate them having the courage to tell us what we need to know
* Thank people

After you listen to the feedback, it's common courtesy to say "Thank you." After you've asked, there's an expectation that you'll listen. After you listen to the feedback, it's common courtesy to say "Thank you." Consider the feedback (feedforward) a GIFT in helping you improve.

It's also a good idea to use the person's name, when saying thank you. Of course, in some cultures, using the first name may not be appropriate. But if you know the person well enough, you should say, "Thank you, Bob."

Let's look at a little example: You're checking out at the grocery store. Doesn't the person usually have a little badge on with a name? If you say, "Thank you, Jim...," notice the change in that person's demeanor. What does he do right away? He looks at you. He thinks you know him. So saying "Thank you" for something that's a gift is important.

What are some of the things you want to avoid when saying "Thank you"?
a) Being insincere
b) Demonstrating impatience or anger

How will you know you're being successful at thanking people? When the desired effect you have on other people is that they see:
* That you appreciate the feedback or the suggestions
* That you're taking their input seriously
* That you are willing to say: "Thank you"

Step 4 - (Think)

The fourth step in the process of developing ourselves is to think about how to respond to the stakeholders' feedback.

What are some wrong behaviors in response to stakeholder feedback whether you're at home or in the office?
* Yelling
* Screaming
* Ranting
* Raving

When we get angry, it's very difficult to do what (before we talk)?
* Stop
* Take a deep breath
* And think

Why am I Talking

What's the behavior you want to reward? The fact that people are willing to say: "Let me give you some feedback. Let me give you a suggestion." You may agree—you may not agree. But reward their suggestions.

Step 5 - (Responding to Feedback)

How should you respond to feedback? There are 3 guidelines.
* Keep it positive
* Keep it simple

* Keep it focused

* When we get feedback, how do we keep it positive?
- Don't act hurt
- Don't act angry
- Don't act beat up

Here's how to keep it simple: Pick ONE key behavior to change.

What should you ask yourself in order to help you keep it focused?
* "What can I commit to "keep in front of me" for the next year?"
* "What can I keep in focus?"
* "What am I willing to *do*, in order to create positive change for myself and the most important people in my life?"

Try to complete this program with goals that actually get accomplished, not "New Year's resolutions" that look good on paper but never really happen.

When responding to positive feedback:
* Don't use the word "but"
Reason: What you say after "but" expresses your critique or judgment of the stakeholder's positive feedback and disregard of everything said previously. Use the word "and." What you say after "and" expresses that you desire more improvement—in addition what the stakeholder has positively appraised.

Here's an example of how to use the word "and" to express that you desire more improvement after receiving positive feedback from a stakeholder.

* Say: "AND there's something I want to improve. I'd like to be more open-minded, a better listener... hear other people's ideas more and focused on my own less. I try to win too much, especially small arguments. I'm going to ask you to help me.
* "The first thing I'd like to say is, I can't change the past. Any mistakes I've made in the past... please accept my apologies. There are no excuses for this behavior. I'm sorry.
* "I can change the future. If you happen to have a couple of ideas, not to talk about the past, but to help me in the future, what would they be?"

(Then, you need to sit there, be quiet, listen, take notes, and say, "Thank you.")

Here is an example of how to respond correctly to stakeholder feedback (that is, how to thank boss, direct reports, colleagues):

Mr. Co-worker, I just went through this 360-degree feedback process. And they asked us to talk to people about what we learned. First thing I'd like to say is that this is a great idea. I love to participate in stuff like this. I have very little to lose and a lot to gain.

The next thing I'd like to say is "thank you" for participating. I know you're busy. I appreciate you taking the time. Also, I'd like to say, "thank you" for all the positive feedback I received. Ethics, dedication, hard work, caring about our company and our customers-- these are important values to me.

Here is a key point that is not usually taught:

When people give us their feedback (feedforward) ideas, we shouldn't judge or critique their ideas in any way... even a positive way. It shows that you're not listening to their ideas

and that you're evaluating and appraising them. The key is not to critique since it adds no value and has a high likelihood of negative value.

Here's an example Marshall uses:
Let's say you give me 3 ideas. The first idea, I say: "That's a great idea!" Second idea: "That's a good idea." Third idea-- nothing.
What message did you just get back from me about your ideas?
1--"A"
2--"C"
3--"F"
Am I listening to your ideas, or am I grading your ideas?
Answer: I'm grading your ideas.

What is the correct way to finish your response to feedback?
* Finish by saying: "I cannot promise to do everything you suggest. I'm going to talk to a lot of people, and I can't promise to do everything everyone suggests.

* "I <u>can</u> promise to listen, to think about your ideas, and to do what I can. And I'm going to ask you to help me in the future. I'm going to follow up with you. And I really appreciate you trying to help me get better at this one item. Thank you very much."

We <u>can't</u> promise to do everything people suggest, and we shouldn't. Leadership isn't a popularity contest. We should let people know that we commit to listening and thinking about their ideas. Then we should just do what we can do.

Step 6 - Involve Others

What does it mean to involve your "key stakeholders"? We'll illustrate with an example:

Let's say that you decide that you're going to delegate more effectively. You've gotten information that you're a micro-manager, and that's what you work on.

You say: "I want to delegate more effectively."

As a coach working with a person, I'm going to ask:

"Who are the 8 or 10 people around you that will know if you've delegated more effectively?"

They will become the people, at the 5 and the 12-month mark, in a little mini-survey, that will determine whether or not you have improved at delegating, and become a more effective delegator with them.

The coach doesn't determine the improvement.
The leader doesn't determine the improvement.
Others determine the improvement.

In order to be an influential leader, you have to have people who are willing to follow.

So that's the systems approach that explains why the stakeholders are critical in this process. The suggestions the stakeholders gave you that you executed on will bring the most positive feelings from the people around you.

So involving the stakeholders in changing behavior and perception in parallel serves another extremely important purpose.

It's critical that they have an opportunity to see the effort you put in to change your leadership behavior.

A big part of your job is making sure your stakeholders are aware of the change as you improve, so that you get credit for it. So make sure to involve those people who were nice enough to give you feedback. Ask THEM to help you change. This is the start of the follow-up process.

Ask key stakeholder(s) to keep you informed on how well you're doing in regards to your request for feedback.

Step 7 - Change

You need to change. You have to go out and do something different based upon the feedback and suggestions you got.

Step 8 - Follow-up

You have to follow up and stick with it. What does follow-up sound like?
"Six weeks ago, I said I wanted to be a better listener.

Based on my behavior during the last six weeks, give me a couple of ideas to help me do better in the next six.

What would they be?"

How often should follow-up be done? About once every 4 to 6 weeks. Go back and talk to each one of your key stakeholders with a simple comment.

The leader should say this: "Six weeks ago, I said I wanted to be a better listener. Based on my behavior during the last six weeks, give me a couple of ideas to help me do better in the next six. What would they be?"

Sit there, be quiet, listen, take notes, and say "Thank you." Follow-up, follow-up, follow-up... every 4-6 weeks!

Feedback or coaching by telephone works about as well as feedback or coaching in person. Frequency of interaction with co-workers and coaches seems to be more important than duration of interaction. Part of the coach's role during this time is to make sure others see the change. Also, the coached person should make sure by his questions that the others see the change. "Have you noticed a difference? Please let me know."

Should the coaches be internal or external to the person's organization? It doesn't matter.

Follow-up with leaders does not have to be a costly tool. Internal coaches can make follow-up telephone calls.

New computerized systems can send "reminder notes" and give ongoing suggestions. Almost any follow-up is better than none.

One of the great weaknesses in most training and development is the insufficient attention paid to follow-up.

Many companies spend millions of dollars for the "program of the year" and almost nothing on the follow-up that can help ensure that the program actually gets executed.

Which is more important in the follow-up process: how often co-workers and coaches interact... or how long they interact? Frequency of interaction with co-workers and coaches seems to be more important than duration of interaction.

The "personal trainer" example seems very applicable to the role of executive coach. The role of the personal trainer is to "remind" the person being trained to do what he/she knows should be done. Most personal trainers spend far less time on theory than they do on execution. The same seems to be true for leadership development. Many leaders know what to do. They have all read the same books and listened to the same "gurus" giving the same speeches.

 <u>Most leaders' biggest challenge is not understanding the practice of leadership; it is practicing their understanding of leadership.</u>

***

Research Study On The Importance Of Follow-up

A research study was conducted in eight organizations here in the U.S and abroad.

The importance of follow-up was a critical element both internationally and domestically.

Approximately 10,000 of the respondents in the eight organizations were located outside of the United States. The importance of follow-up was as critical to changing behavior internationally as it was domestically. This was true for both training and coaching initiatives.

While the concept of follow-up and frequency were universal, leaders were encouraged to adapt their follow-up message to fit the unique requirements of their culture. This was especially true when leadership development was involved. The concepts and learnings were applicable to all of the countries that the training was conducted in but it was important to get the involvement of participants in helping mold these concepts and learnings to fit the unique circumstances and customs of their countries.

A common belief is that feedback or coaching is a very "personal" activity and that it is much more effective if done in person (as opposed to by phone). Research conducted by these eight organizations does not support this belief. The organization that conducted almost all feedback by telephone produced almost identical "increased effectiveness" scores as the organization that conducted all feedback in person. The organizations that used all external coaches made sure that each coach had at least two "one-on-one" meetings with his/her client. Some coaches met with clients regularly in person, while some had almost all interaction by telephone. There was no clear indication that either method of coaching was superior to the other.

One client did a "client satisfaction" study comparing client satisfaction with 360° feedback by telephone vs. feedback in person. Clients were equally satisfied with either process. While this type of "happiness measure" is not as valid as long-term measures, it shows that even the short-term experience of feedback by telephone can be as positive as the experience of feedback in person.

In company "H" only external coaches were used. In company "B" only internal coaches were used. Both approaches produced very positive, long-term results in increasing leadership effectiveness. The three major variables in determining whether to use an internal or external coach seemed to be *time, credibility* and *confidentiality*.

In company "B" internal coaches were given the time to do the job. This was treated as an important part of their responsibility, not an "add on" to do "if they got around to it". They were trained in the coaching process and viewed as highly credible by their internal clients. (In fact, their internal clients said they preferred them to external coaches.) Each internal coach worked with a leader in a different part of the business. They assured their clients that this process was for high-potential development, not evaluation.

In many organizations, internal coaches just do not have the time to interact with a meaningful sample of leaders on an ongoing basis. In some cases they may not seem as credible to executives. In other cases they may appear to be in a "conflict of interest" position in terms of their role as a coach and their role as an evaluator. If these perceptions exist, then external coaches may be preferable.

Internal coaches were seen as having the advantage of "knowing the business" and "understanding the key players". External coaches were seen as having the advantage of an "outside perspective" and "objectivity". Neither choice seemed to be "better" or "worse" in an absolute sense. The appropriate answer appears to depend upon the unique needs and resources of the organization.

Companies "A" and "G" provided training on how to involve co-workers in follow-up and continuous improvement. Leaders also received ongoing "reminder notes", suggesting that they should follow-up. With today's new technology, very sophisticated follow-up systems are available to help ensure that follow-up occurs. As a rule, the more that the company follows-up with the leader, the more the leader follows-up with the co-workers (and the more effective the leader becomes).

One reason that coaching is so effective is that it helps inspire leaders to follow-up with their people. Company "H" found a strong positive correlation between the number of times that the coach followed-up with the client and the number of times that the client followed-up with co-workers.

Follow-up with leaders does not have to be a costly tool. Internal coaches can make follow-up telephone calls. New computerized systems can send "reminder notes" and give ongoing suggestions. Almost any follow-up is better than none. One of the great weaknesses in most training and development is the insufficient attention paid to follow-up. Many companies spend millions of dollars for the "program of the year" and almost nothing on the follow-up that can help ensure that the program actually gets executed!

Frequency of interaction with co-workers and coaches seems to be more important than duration of interaction.

In all eight companies the frequency of interaction seemed to be a major variable. All companies noted that frequency of interaction with co-workers was a key driver of success. As was mentioned earlier, Company "H" also mentioned that frequency of interaction with coaches made a positive difference.

Historically, a great deal of leadership development has focused on the importance of an *event*. This event could be a training program, a motivational speech or and executive off-site meeting. The experience of these eight companies indicates that real leadership development is a *process*.

A good analogy might be working out. The historical approach to leadership development would be to have leaders sit in a room and watch demonstrations on how to exercise. The company would then wonder why everyone was not in shape a year later! Arnold Schwarzenegger wisely said, "Nobody ever got muscles by watching *me* work out." The key to getting in shape is not one's understanding the theory of working out. It is engaging in the process of working out!

The "personal trainer" example seems very applicable to the role of executive coach. The role of the personal trainer is to "remind" the person being trained to do what he/she knows should be done. Most personal trainers spend far less time on theory than they do on execution. The same seems to be true for leadership development. Many leaders know what to do. They have all read the same books and listened to the same "gurus" giving the same speeches. *Most leaders biggest challenge is not understanding the practice of leadership; it is practicing their understanding of leadership.*

One lesson is clear from the six companies in our study that included training programs. *If leaders go to a leadership development program, and do not follow-up with their people, they might as well stay home.* While there is some evidence that coaching without follow-up can produce some positive change in leadership behavior (from Company "H"), there is no evidence that training without follow-up can produce positive change in leadership behavior that is any greater than "random chance".

***

Most people want to think: "I'll just change, and they'll notice it." They don't! So the key is getting people to ask, "Have you noticed a difference?" The first time you ask the stakeholder that, most people will say, "I can't really say that I have." It's a wakeup call for <u>them</u>. You've done some things… they haven't noticed.

You're not there to get upset. You should just say, "Okay. I'm going to ask you next month if you've noticed a difference. Please let me know." Because, remember, one of the goals we're working at here is changing behavior and perception. And your role as a coach is to make sure that the people that you're coaching understands that part of their role is to get people to see the change—or they won't see it. They just won't see it! When people don't get the improvement they hoped for, they're angry, they're upset. Because they <u>have</u> made the effort and they <u>have</u> changed. But what they haven't done is taken the time to make sure that the person has seen it.

<u>Example Question:</u> What principle does this excerpt illustrate?
"It also gives people the impression you don't value R and D (Research and Development) as much as I know you do."
"I was really just trying to be light-hearted."
A) But
B) Follow up
C) Involving other people
Answer: A. He is making an excuse instead of accepting feedback.

To review briefly, the process of developing ourselves is quite simple:
*Figure out a profile of what you want to be.
* Get feedback on "Am I doing it?"
* Develop a plan that's positive, simple, and focused.
* Talk to people around you and involve them.
* Follow up (by giving a couple of mini-surveys) maybe once every six months.

Secrets of a Leadership Coach 3 Developing Others

In this course we will answer the following questions:
* How do I help another person achieve a positive, measurable change in his or her behavior?
* What are the steps in the coaching process?

Here are the eight steps to coach others to improve their behavior:
Step 1 Identify desired behaviors
Step 2 Choose the raters
Step 3 Collect feedback
Step 4 Analyze Results (Pick One Key Behavior)
Step 5 Develop an Action Plan
Step 6 Have Person Respond to Key Stakeholders
Step 7 Ongoing Follow-up & Mini-survey
Step 8 Review Results & Start Again

You may be asking yourself, "But I'm not a professional trainer. We have people who do that! Why do I need to learn executive coaching?"

Answer: A manager is also a coach. This course teaches managers how to be executive coaches.

What does it take to be a good coach? As a parent, you're also in the role of a coach. How do you help your children improve? What are some of the skills to be a good coach? You have to be good at helping the person you're working with set good behavioral goals. The two key categories are:
1) Help the people you're coaching fit the coaching to their personal needs and connect it to their wider world.

2) Keep the diagnosis of their behavior balanced. You don't always have to focus on weaknesses. Sometimes your biggest improvement will be because you focused on one of their strengths.

Behavioral Coaching

Are there situations where behavioral coaching won't work?

Absolutely. Don't use this tool in any of the following circumstances:
* The person isn't willing to try.
* The person is written off by the company (that means he or she doesn't have a chance).
* Functional, technical or strategic problems. (Behavioral coaching only solves behavioral problems. It doesn't make a bad strategy a good one.)
* The person is headed in the wrong direction, or has an integrity or ethics issue. (If a person has an ethics issue, fire him or her. Don't use behavioral coaching.)
When will behavioral coaching work?
* If, and only if, 3 conditions exist:
    1. The issue is behavioral
    2. The person is motivated to change
    3. The person is given a chance
These conditions usually exist for 60% of all requests for behavioral coaching.

How does the coaching process work, in general?
* Have the successful person receive feedback on important, self-selected behaviors as perceived by stakeholders selected by the person and verified by his, or her, manager.

A co-worker, spouse, partner, or significant other who has no interest in changing can't be changed. You just can't change another adult person who resists change. So STOP – Trying to *make* successful people change.

Trying To Change Person Resistant To Change

Have you ever attempted to change the behavior of a successful adult who had absolutely no interest in changing? How much luck did you have in this "religious conversion" activity? I have asked these questions to thousands of leaders and their answers are almost always the same, "Yes, I have tried and no, I didn't have any luck!"

How much of our lives have been invested in attempting to change the behavior of adults that have no interest in changing? What is our return on this investment? The most common answers are "Too much and it did more harm than good!"

How many years have you invested in attempting to change the behavior of a spouse, significant other or partner that had no interest in changing? What was your return on that investment? The answer to the first question obviously varies by age and marital status. The most common answer to the second question is, "It definitely wasn't worth it!"

An example from Marshall's personal life:

My mother was an excellent first grade school teacher. Mom lived in an entire world that was populated by first graders. I was always in the first grade. My father was in the first grade. All of our relatives were in the first grade. Mom was always correcting everyone's grammar. One day she was correcting

Dad (for about the thousandth time). He looked at her, sighed, and said, "Honey, I'm 70 years old. Let it go."

One organization that understands this very well is Alcoholics Anonymous. People who participate in AA begin discussions with one sentence – only four words – I am an alcoholic. They have learned through years of experience that if a people are unwilling to admit they have problems, they will not change their behavior.

Step 1 Identify desired behaviors
Involve the person in identifying the desired behaviors for a person in his or her position. Before we do behavioral coaching, the person needs to get a good grasp of what is desired behavior.

Step 2 Choose the raters
Choose the raters. Involve the person in determining who can give him or her meaningful feedback.

Why do successful people deny the validity of feedback?
* 1) Wrong questions. (This is why you should involve them in figuring out what the right behaviors or questions are.)
* 2) Wrong raters. (This is why you should involve them in picking the raters.)

The reasons why you should involve successful people in figuring out what the right behaviors or questions are:
* The more they are involved in determining what this desired behavior is, the more likely they are to "buy in" to the validity of demonstrating this behavior.
* Successful people are very responsive to help in achieving goals that they have set.

* They tend to resist changes that make them feel "judged" or "manipulated."

The reasons why you should involve successful people in picking the raters are:
* It is very difficult for a person to deny the validity of feedback when he or she picks the behaviors and the raters.
* If successful people select the raters, they will be much more likely to accept the validity of the feedback. Most executives respect the opinion of *almost all* of their key colleagues.
* By letting the successful person pick the raters, you can avoid the potential reaction, "Why should a winner like me listen to a loser like him?"

The Reasons Why It's Best To Involve Successful People In Picking Both The Behaviors And The Raters

It is hard to measure effectiveness in changing behavior unless there is a clear agreement on what desired behavior is. Successful people have a high need for self-determination. Ultimately, the ownership of the behavioral change process will have to come from the people who are changing their behavior, not from an internal or external coach.

One reason that successful people tend to deny the validity of behavioral feedback is that they were not involved in determining the desired behavior for a person in their position. The more they are involved in determining what this desired behavior is, the more likely they are to "buy in" to the validity of demonstrating this behavior. Successful people are very responsive to help in achieving goals that they have set. They tend to resist changes that make them feel "judged" or "manipulated."

Successful people also have a desire for internal consistency. If leaders publicly state that certain behavior is important, they will be more likely to strive to be a positive role model in demonstrating this behavior.

From my experience in developing leadership profiles, I have found that almost all executives will develop a great profile of their "desired" behaviors. In most cases, understanding what behaviors are desired will not be their major challenge. Their major challenge will be demonstrating these behaviors.

An example of the value of involving leaders in developing their own profile occurred with a CEO client several years ago. When he received feedback from his co-workers (on his own behavior), he looked skeptically at one of the lower scoring items and asked, "Who was the person that wanted to include that item?" I replied, "You!" He then remembered why he wanted to include the item. He also began to face the fact that the real problem was his own behavior, not the wording of an item.

The first reason that people deny the validity of behavioral feedback is "wrong behaviors." The second reason is "wrong raters." If successful people select the raters, they will be much more likely to accept the validity of the feedback. Most executives respect the opinion of almost all of their key colleagues. By letting the successful person pick the raters, you can avoid the potential reaction, "Why should a winner like me listen to a loser like him?"

One argument against letting the people we coach pick their own raters is that they will pick their "friends" and the feedback will not be representative. I have not found this to be true for two reasons: 1) Almost all of the executives I have met end up selecting raters that are similar to the group I would select anyway. The only time they do not want to include someone is if the person is about to leave the company or they have a deep disrespect for this person. In my experience, I have never had an executive want to exclude more than two raters. 2) When 360° feedback is used for developmental purposes, the "items for improvement" that emerge from self-selected raters are quite similar to the items that come from other-selected raters.

Step 3 Collect Feedback

Collect feedback. Just as in self-development, encourage people to give their feedback in the form of feedforward.

Just as in self-development, encourage people to give their feedback in the form of feedforward. A racecar driver has an analogy: Look at the road, don't look at the wall. The whole idea of feedforward is this: Focus on the future; don't focus on the past.

How do you get the feedback from the key stakeholder?

Just talk to him or her. All you say is this:
* "I want to be a better leader."
* "I can't change the past."
* "If you have a couple of ideas on how I could be a better leader in the future, what would they be?"

What should you do next?

Use feedforward to identify areas to work on:
* Pick one behavior you want to change

* Ask people for ideas about the future, not feedback about the past
* Don't judge or critique people's ideas
* Listen to their ideas
* Take notes about what they say
* Come up with a plan

The main problem with regular feedback is that it focuses on a *past* - that cannot be changed - not a *future* that can be changed. In this sense, feedback can be limited and static, as opposed to expansive and dynamic.

Over the past several years, Marshall has observed more than five thousand leaders as they participated in a fascinating experiential exercise.

In the exercise, participants are each asked to play two roles.
* In one role, they are asked to provide feedforward—that is, to give someone else suggestions for the future and *help as much as they can.*
* In the second role, they are asked to accept feedforward—that is, to listen to the suggestions for the future and *learn as much as they can.*

The exercise typically lasts for 10-15 minutes, and the average participant has 6-7 dialogue sessions. In the exercise participants are asked to:
* Pick one behavior that they would like to change. *Change in this behavior should make a significant, positive difference in their lives.*
* Describe this behavior to randomly selected fellow participants. *This is done in one-on-one dialogues. It can be done quite simply, such as, "I want to be a better listener."*

* Ask for feedforward—for two suggestions for the future that might help them achieve a positive change in their selected behavior. *If participants have worked together in the past, they are not allowed to give ANY feedback about the past. They are only allowed to give ideas for the future.*
* Listen attentively to the suggestions and take notes. *Participants are not allowed to comment on the suggestions in any way. They are not allowed to critique the suggestions or even to make positive judgmental statements, such as, "That's a good idea."*
* Thank the other participants for their suggestions.
* Ask the other persons what they would like to change.
* Provide feedforward - two suggestions aimed at helping them change.
* Say, "You are welcome." when thanked for the suggestions. *The entire process of both giving and receiving feedforward usually takes about two minutes.*
* Find another participant and keep repeating the process until the exercise is stopped.

This exercise is seen as fun and helpful as opposed to painful, embarrassing, or uncomfortable.

Step 4 Analyze Results (Pick One Key Behavior)

* Pick one that's most important
* Fix that
* Let go of the rest

Step 5 Develop an Action Plan

* Help the person develop an action plan.

* This not only involves the person being coached, but that person's key stakeholders. This includes his or her co-workers and the other people around the person as well.

In doing behavioral coaching, more than half of the coach's job is NOT spent with the person being coached. It's spent with the people around the person being coached: the key stakeholders.

What does the coach do with the person's key stakeholders?

At the beginning of the process, Marshall tells each of the coached person's key stakeholders: "Joe (Jill), I'm going to be working with your manager. And the way I work is that I don't get paid if you don't get better. And 'better' is not going to be determined by him or me; it's going to be determined by you."

As a coach, Marshall requests three main things from the key stakeholders.

1. The first request is:
* "Can you let go of the past?"
* "Whatever real or imagined sins he's committed in the past, I can't fix, and he can't fix."
* "If you bring up the past, you only demoralize people."

2. The second request the coach makes to the key stakeholders is:
* Be honest.
* I'm going to hand you forms to fill out.
* I want you to swear to me you're going to tell the truth. Don't be too positive, and don't be too negative.
* And the only person to judge the truth about your opinion is you.

3. The third request that Marshall (or any leadership coach) makes to each key stakeholder is:
* Can you promise to me to be a helpful and supportive coach to this other person (your boss), and not a cynic, critic, or judge?
* Because if he (she) tries to get better and all he hears back from you is cynicism or criticism, he gives up!

Ninety-eight percent of the people that Marshall makes these three requests to say "yes."

Occasionally, they say: "No, I can't forgive the person; I can't let go of the past."

What do you think Marshall says to these people (and what should <u>any</u> coach say)?
* "Thank you. I'm going to hand you a form, like everybody else. I just have one request... when you get the form, please throw it away."
* "Because, wouldn't you agree... it's not fair for you to judge another person, when you've already told me you're not going to give him a chance?"

Successful people attribute more validity to the sincere recognition of success than to the sincere acknowledgement of failure. Behavioral change is almost always "non-linear". Almost all adults will have "setbacks" when attempting to change behavior.

Co-workers need to realize that this is a natural part of the process and not "give up" on the executive. We all have a tendency to revert back to behaviors that were correlated with success in the past. The more successful we are, the easier it is to rationalize this return to past behavior.

If the executive is encouraged to move beyond setbacks and the colleagues do not dwell on these setbacks, the odds for long-term change greatly improve. The colleague's goal should be to help the executive feel like a "winner" as they participate in the process of change.

Step 6 Have Person Respond to Key Stakeholders

How should this be done?
* In a positive, simple, and focused way.
* Just say: "Thank you for helping me. Here's what I've learned. Here's what I'm going to do better. I feel very positive about the good stuff... here's the one thing I'm going to improve."
* And have them ask each of their key stakeholders: "How can I be better in the future?"

As a leader or manager, as a person trying to help others change, here's a guideline:
* Don't be the only coach.
* Create an environment where every person around the individual becomes the coach... not just you.

Review Question: Which of the following is NOT true?
a) The person's key stakeholders all become the coach.
b) An environment should be created in which every person around the individual becomes the coach.
c) The leadership coach should be the only person who even knows about the leader's decision to attempt a behavioral change.
Answer: c.

Step 7 Ongoing Follow-up & Mini-survey

The next step is to develop an on-going follow-up and mini-survey process.

Have that person you're coaching go back to each key stakeholder on a regular basis (maybe once a month) and say:

"I said I wanted to be a better listener.

"Based on my behavior last month, what ideas do you have for me next month?"

Develop a follow-up process that provides an opportunity for ongoing dialogue on selected behaviors with selected colleagues. These follow-up dialogues are very focused and need take only a few minutes. They can be done by phone or in-person.

A mini-survey might say:
"In the past six months, has this person become more effective or less effective as a listener?"

Mini-surveys are not complex, and again, they don't have to be long. They could be one item... or four items.

It's important to keep the survey short. Then the person can get some very quick mini-survey feedback that people don't see as a constraint or a waste of time.

People are sick of filling out 80-item forms and 120-item forms. They're not sick of filling out one-to-four-item forms.

What are specific reasons why mini-surveys can be a simple and efficient way to measure behavioral change?
* Besides typically being very short, mini-surveys usually focus only on the behaviors that have been selected by the person being coached.
* They are designed so that the raters evaluate behavior that occurs *only* during the coaching period.
* They focus on the rater's perception of *improvement*.

What must the executive (or other person) do to almost always guarantee that a positive change will occur?

The coached person must:
* Agree upon the desired behaviors for change
* Select highly respected co-workers as raters
* Take the process seriously and follow up

THE RESULT:
* Positive change will almost always occur

What should the person do after receiving the mini-survey results?
* Thank the raters
* Involve them in future change
* Continue the process

This is almost always a positive experience for both the executive and for the co-workers.

Step 8 Review Results & Start Again

To review briefly, the coaching process is simple:
* Figure out a profile of what the coached person wants to be.
* Help that person get feedback on "Is he or she is doing it?"

* Help the person develop a plan that's positive, simple, and focused.
* Have the person talk to his surrounding people and involve them.
* Have the person follow up (by giving a couple of mini-surveys), maybe once every six months.

The person almost always achieves a positive, measurable change in behavior.

How does the coached person know when he's successful in the follow up process?
-When other people see his eagerness for suggestions
-When other people see he has learned
-When other people see he has executed on what he has said he would get better at

Other people have to see the change; otherwise you don't get credit for it. That is one of the key principles: Change behavior and perception in parallel. That's why the last step (the follow up) is the most important.

Role Play #1: Responding To Feedback

Coach: "NAME, now that we've discussed the suggestions from your stakeholders and developed a plan using some of these suggestions, it is time to respond to your stakeholders. Let me give you an example of what I mean and then let's practice right here. O.K.?"

Leader: "Sounds good to me."

Coach: "How to respond to your direct reports will be something like this:

I really appreciate all the comments and suggestions I have received regarding my goal of improving my delegating. This process has really been beneficial. What I have chosen to work on first is more clearly defining what the success measures as I delegate tasks. Would you be willing to give me feedback on whether I'm doing this over the coming months? Now you do it."

Leader: "I really appreciate all the comments and suggestions I have received regarding my goal of improving my delegating. This process has really been beneficial. *All of the suggestions were really great.* What I have chosen to work on first is more clearly defining what the success measures as I delegate tasks. Would you be willing to give me feedback on whether I'm doing this over the coming months?"

Coach: "You almost got it right. What did you do differently from what I suggested?"

Leader: [Reflecting] "I'm not sure."

<u>YOUR TURN</u>: Which phrase represents the INCORRECT change from what the coach asked the leader to do?
A) I really appreciate all the comments and suggestions I have received regarding my goal of improving my delegating. This process has really been beneficial.
B) All of the suggestions were really great.
C) What I have chosen to work on first is more clearly defining the success measures as I delegate tasks.
D) Would you be willing to give me feedback on whether I'm doing this over the coming months?
<u>Answer:</u> B

Coach: "You critiqued the suggestions. After you said the process has been very beneficial, you said the suggestions were all very beneficial. That is not an accurate statement and may lead to some unintended consequences down the road. Remember we don't want to come across as grading the suggestions, good, bad, or indifferent. Let's try it again?"

Leader: "O.K."

Coach: [Out of the role play] "As a coach, one of your most useful tools is behavioral rehearsal. This process prepares the person to have a conversation that achieves the desired effect and to avoid certain actions that may be counterproductive."

Role Play #2: Follow-up
Leader: "I'm feeling a bit funny checking in with my folks. I've been doing this for months now and most of what I'm getting is reinforcement that I'm doing a good job of listening to others' points of view. It makes me feel like I'm fishing for compliments."

Coach: "Remember, changing your behavior is not the toughest part. Changing their perception is. Let me give you an example. You go to a restaurant and get lousy service and lousy food. You vow never to go back. So, you keep driving by and don't go back, right?"

Leader: "Right."

Coach: "Say the restaurant failed because of the lousy food and service. It goes under. New management takes over and put in a great chef and likeable, well-trained professional waiters. The place has become a fabulous restaurant.

"You, on the other hand, drive by and won't give it another chance…unless you see a banner displayed outside the restaurant that says: Under New Management.

"What you are doing with this monthly follow-up is putting out the banner. See my point?"

Leader: "Got it! They have to see the change for me to get the real payoff."

Coach: "Exactly, our perceptions are our reality."

Coach: [Out of role] "Changing behavior is only half the game.

"Others have to see the change in effect before they will recognize it.

"Follow-up is the key."

Secrets of a Leadership Coach 4 Developing a Team

Upon the completion of this course, you will be able to...
1. Identify why team building is important
2. Analyze the steps in the team-building process
3. Give examples of team areas for behavioral change
4. Describe individual areas for behavioral change
5. Describe communication methods for follow-up

First, team building is more important than ever. Why?
* More and more, one manages knowledge workers.
* The people in teams are spread out around the world.

* Synergy has become both more important and more difficult because there's never enough time.

That's why this process is called "Team building without time wasting."

You can do it very quickly.

Step #1 of the Team Building Process

The first question to ask a group of people is:

"Do you need to work together as a team, yes or no?" If the answer is yes, then the second question is, "Do you just work together, and you're interdependent… but not really a team working toward a common goal?"
If the answer to the question is yes, a second question to ask is:

"On a scale of 1 to 10, how well are you working together as a team now?" (10 being fabulous, 1 being abysmal, 5 being right around in the middle.)
Everybody puts their individual score on a piece of paper, you collect them, divide them by the number of people in the group and you come up with a team score.

Step #2 of the Team Building Process

Then you ask the group a second question: "How well do we need to work together as a team?" (On a scale of 1 to 10)

Doing this reveals an interesting gap analysis (the difference between what they are and what they want to be).

They've said that they're a team, and they've said that they need to work better together, and they've said this is how they're working now.

What's the typical answer? Over 1000 Fortune 500 teams say: "We are a 5.8, but we wish we were an 8.7." Most of us don't feel our teams are working together as well as we should.

Step #3 of the Team Building Process

Now you get them to self-select a behavior:
What's a behavior, that if they all did it, if they ALL did it, would significantly improve how this team is working?

Say to everybody on the team: "Okay, team... if we could all pick two behaviors... and if everybody got better at these two things, it would improve the quality of teamwork…What would they be?"

You can use the results of a group 360 and then use the group technique to come up with a behavior that everybody agrees would significantly improve how the team works—if they all did it better.

* Everybody writes them down, and then you pick a couple of behaviors. (Marshall's bias now is to pick only one behavior to try to change.)
* And then you prioritize.

Step #4 of the Team Building Process

Next, have each person get an individual behavior to change.

And the way you do this is simple:

Each person talks to every other person on the team in a one-on-one dialogue that only takes a minute.
* What's one thing (or two things) I can do better to help the team?

Step #5 of the Team Building Process

Now we begin the follow-up process.

Once a month, each team member has a very quick follow-up with each other team member that only takes a second. The medium of communication is not important; the message is.

"Our team area for improvement is listening.

"Based on my behavior last month, if you had an idea to help me this month, what would it be?

"Thank you."

Then take notes... follow up, and keep following up.

"My own area for behavioral improvement is communicating the goals of our organization.

"Based on my behavior last month, if you had an idea to help me this month, what would it be?

"Thank you."

Take notes... follow up, and keep following up.

In about six months, use a team-specific mini-survey.

What's the best way to do that?
* Pick <u>one</u> team item and <u>one</u> individual item.
* Discuss the results
* Restart the process

<u>Step #6</u>

Restart the process.

<u>Review Question</u> on Team Building: Which of the following is NOT correct for developing a team?
A) "So my understanding is that each member of the senior team will work on supporting the final decision of the team back to their team once it's been made."
B) "Each individual on the senior team will have their own individual behavior."
C) "For the team behavior, we have decided it doesn't make sense to have one single behavior everyone works on.
Answer: C.

<u>Challenges to Changing</u>

Of course, some leaders (or team members) may not like the process. Since change is often difficult, it may not be pleasant in the immediate sense.

But as a true leader, you must distinguish between doing what you like to do—and doing what you know is necessary.

And a leader has to execute the process systematically, being careful not to confuse learning with knowledge, or knowledge with wisdom.

The members of the teams need to have individual commitments to making an improvement for the whole team. Commitment to the process means:
1) A person has the desire to get better
2) That person has the discipline

The coach should ask, "On a scale of 1 to 10, how important is this improvement to you?" If they say, "6," then the coach should say, "Well, let me help you get it to an 8." If they can't give the answer, then the coach has to question their commitment to the process.

And, in fact, in this executive coaching process, the coach is not described or represented as some all-wise, all-knowing guru coach.

This process is unique in that the team involves its members in a systems approach.

And so all team members need to ask themselves:
"Is it important to them?"
"Is it important to me?"
"What are the benefits to me if I become better at _____ (e.g., delegating more effectively?"

And if you can't come up with the benefits for that, you can take a lot of classes and a lot of courses… but improvement probably won't be the result.

Changing and Assessment

It's important for the team to do what's called an "after-action assessment."

There are 4 key questions.
1) What did we set out to do?
2) What actually happened?
3) Why did it happen?
4) What are we going to do next time?

This should be done with successes as well as failures. The most common excuse for not doing it is, "I'm too busy."

Each team member's change must be made visible to others in the team. How do you know you're successful at following up? When <u>other people</u> start to see you eager for their suggestions. They see that you've actually learned through this process. And that you've actually executed on what it is you said you were going to get better at.

Change behavior and change perception in parallel. It is important for the members of the team to notice that the other team members have changed and that the team as a whole has changed.

Secrets of a Leadership Coach 5 Practice and Assessments

This guidebook will take you through the development of your personal action plan for each of the first four parts of the series separately:

Secrets of a Leadership Coach 1 Executive Coaching Techniques
Secrets of a Leadership Coach 2 Developing Ourselves as Leaders
Secrets of a Leadership Coach 3 Developing Others

Important note that applies to all the examples given here: Sometimes the sample statements made seem rather strong, as if the person speaking has been horrid. Those sample statements are strong in order to make the point. In practice (we hope), you have much more minor issues to work on, and you can tone down the statements accordingly.

Regard this manual as a workbook. We have left space for you to enter your own ideas and phrases.

SECRETS OF A LEADERSHIP COACH 1 EXECUTIVE COACHING TECHNIQUES

Feedforward is crucial to the concept of coaching.

The first thing you need to do is identify your problem.

What can I commit to "keep in front of me" for the next year?

_____

What can I keep in focus?

_____

What am I willing to *do*, in order to create positive change for myself and the most important people in my life?

_____

Now look over what you wrote above in the three questions, and write down the things you want to work on, in order of importance.

_____

Enter the phrase you think you should use with a co-worker to ask for his feedforward on your problem.

I want to be a
better…_____

After he responds, you say something like this: I'd like two suggestions for the future that would help me make a positive change in my behavior.

_____

How will you react to an insensitive response? Prepare your answer according to this model: You should gently explain to him that the purpose of your asking him is to obtain suggestions for the future. Dwelling on the past won't help. You emphasize that you are aware of your own faults and want to improve.

_____

_____

Now enter your notes about his suggestions:

_____

_____

Write down how you would respond to him. Here is the basic principle: You are not allowed to critique the suggestions or even to make positive judgmental statements, such as, "That's a good idea." Whatever you say, you should start off with "thank you" and, if you want, you could stop with that!

_____

_____

You may often be in the position of giving suggestions to others, or coaching them on how to use feedforward. Feedforward is explained in more detail in previous courses. Basically, it is restricted to giving ideas for future improvement. Contrast the following:

Constructively delivered feedback:
"You would have done a much better job of listening at the last meeting if you didn't complete people's sentences for them."

Feedforward
"You should try not to make any responses to someone's idea until that person has said he's finished explaining it."

Even constructively delivered feedback is often seen as negative as it necessarily involves a discussion of mistakes, shortfalls, and problems.

Feedforward, on the other hand, is almost always seen as positive because it focuses on solutions.

Now you can practice giving feedforward.

Your employee has made a horrible presentation about your newest product. Here is one possible answer: "My suggestion for the future is to take a course on PowerPoint presentations to make sure you are taking full advantage of all the program's features to help you make a perfect presentation."

Here is a model of how to preface those comments. Think about it and then write down one that sounds right for you: "Here are four ideas for the future. Please accept these in the positive spirit that they are given. If you can only use two of the ideas, you are still two ahead. Just ignore what doesn't make sense for you."

_____

_____

_____

_____

_____

_____

Here are some common problems of leaders. Identify which of those apply to you. Use the space below to develop some ways you feel comfortable asking for feedforward about these issues.
- Trying to win too much.
- Impatience
- Not letting other people finish a sentence
- Figuring out what other people have to say before they say it
- Trying to be right too much.
- Not treating people with enough respect
- Coming across to people as arrogant or opinionated

Here are the things that Marshall makes a leader commit to as part of the behavior improvement process. Use these to make yourself a short speech that YOU feel comfortable saying to someone you work with in the space below.

- Commit to getting feedback.
  - Commit to, and publicly identify, the behaviors to work on.
  - Commit to having one-on-one dialogues with each of the people who are significant stakeholders.
  - Apologize for previous mistakes.
  - Say you are not going to make excuses for your previous behavior.
  - Follow up on a regular basis
  - Get re-measured

Here is a model speech: "I am going through this coaching process and I just got some feedback. I really appreciate participating in a process like this. I appreciate the time and the energy you have taken to give me good feedback. The issues you gave feedback on are very meaningful to me. There are a couple of things I would like to improve. *(If you are doing this without a coach, you should revise this appropriately.)*

"One is that I want to do a better job of treating people with respect.

"Also, I may have come across to some people as arrogant or opinionated in the past. If I have ever done that around you please accept my apologies. There is no excuse for this behavior, but I cannot change the past.

"If you have a couple of ideas to help me do a better job of treating people with respect in the future, what would they be?"

We learned in the course that one of the greatest mistakes of successful people is the assumption, "I am successful. I behave this way. Therefore, I must be successful *because* I behave this way!" However, sometimes those people might have been successful *in spite of* something they did.

We will now give you an exercise to examine yourself. This is important because it will open you up to re-evaluating your behaviors. First, a model:

Here is the *"because"* assumption:

"I succeeded at improving corporate efficiency during the recent merger by making everyone scared of not performing and being fired."

This can be thought of differently from an *"in spite of"* perspective:

"I succeeded at improving corporate efficiency during the recent merger in spite of making everyone scared of not performing and being fired. In retrospect, employees might have concentrated on their jobs better if they hadn't spent so much time gossiping about who might be fired next."

Now you edit the statements for yourself:
I succeeded at ... because I...(something positive about yourself).

_____

_____

Now turn your self-congratulatory statement into an "in spite of" statement.
I succeeded at... in spite of.... In retrospect, ...

_____

_____

We all need to work on self-improvement. We often don't work on self-improvement because of overcommitment. Pick something you didn't manage to get done that you wanted to. If you can't think of anything specific, why not choose organizing the papers in your office? Write down an excuse for why you didn't in the space below.

First, read this typical excuse:
"You know, I am incredibly busy right now. In fact, I feel about as busy today as I have ever felt. Some days I feel over-committed. In fact, every now and then my life feels out of control.

"But we are working on some very unique and special challenges right now. I feel like the worst of this is going to be over in a couple of months.

"After that, I am going to take a couple of weeks, take a little time off, get organized, spend some time with the family, and start working out. Everything is going to change. This time will be here soon. After that, it won't be crazy anymore!"

Secrets of a Leadership Coach 2 Developing Ourselves as Leaders

Part 2 of the series was mostly concerned with developing oneself and elaborating on the concept of feedforward. The basic idea is ask, listen, and learn (and apply). The exercises are very similar to those from Part 1 of this series.

Let's start by practicing asking.

First introduce the subject. Here is a good starter sentence:
"I would like to do a better job of listening."
Maybe you would add a preface like, "I've been thinking, and..." That's OK, too.

Now memorize the phrase in quotation marks EXACTLY before proceeding.

First write it down from memory.

Now write it in your own words. It should sound like one of the following:
I would like to do a better job of listening.
I would like to do a better job of listening to other people.
I want to be a better listener.
I would like to be a better listener.

Now you might make an apology. Here is a standard format to use.

"If I have come across as arrogant or opinionated in the past around you please accept my apologies. There is no excuse for this behavior, but I cannot change the past."

Try to memorize this as much as you can. It may be too strong for things you want to fix, so you can tone it down. (For example, "If I have come across in the past as insufficiently sensitive to the feelings of the people around me, please accept my apologies. I'm not making excuses now. I just want your help for the future.") Enter an apology to follow the introduction to explain how you feel bad about not having listened.

Now enter how YOU would phrase an apology for the issue you have chosen to work with.

There are a few similar ways to ask for feedforward:
"Would you be willing to give me a few ideas on how to treat people better?"
"If you have a couple of ideas to help me do a better job of treating people with respect in the future, what would they be?"
"How can I treat people better?"

Now try making a phrase about listening.

Now make a request for feedforward about YOUR own area of concern.

Your asking questions to elicit feedforward is not limited to your publicly confessed problems. You can--and should--get used to asking questions about your performance to all the people you work with. Here is an example:

"I want to be a better supplier. How can I serve you better?"

How would you phrase a request for feedforward from a person who is your vendor?

_____

_____

Now that you have your speech worked out, you need to identify 8-10 people to provide you with feedforward. Include your colleagues, managers, and supervisees. Do that now.

Let us say that you have asked for feedforward, the co-worker gives it to you, and then asks you, "What's your opinion of what I said?" or some similar phrase.

Whatever your answer is, it should include thanks for the help, and appreciation of his having the courage to tell you what to do better. You should avoid completely any response as to whether his comments are right or wrong.

Now write down your response:

SECRETS OF A LEADERSHIP COACH 3 DEVELOPING OTHERS

Part 3 of the series was mostly concerned with developing others.

Your first step as a "coach" is to identify someone worth working with.

The following questions will give you a short tool to help you evaluate whether to spend your time coaching that person.
Is the person unwilling to try?
Has the company written off this person?
Does this person have functional, technical, or strategic problems?
Does the person have an integrity or ethics issue?

If any of the answers are yes, you should consider whether this person is appropriate for coaching.

Now imagine a co-worker that you would like to coach, and enter below what you have decided to coach him on. Pick the behavior that is most important.

You will have to tell the people around the coached person (the stakeholders) to cooperate with you. You need to speak to them in order to gain their support in changing something they may be fed up with. Here is a suggestion of some things to say:

"Joe (Jill), I'm going to be working with your manager. And the way I work is that I don't get paid if you don't get better. And 'better' is not going to be determined by him or me; it's going to be determined by you. Can you let go of the past? Whatever real or imagined sins he's committed in the past, I can't fix, and he can't fix. If you bring up the past, you only demoralize people."

Now try entering your own speech to the stakeholders.

Next you want the stakeholders to fill out initial evaluation forms. They may not want to be bothered. So you have to prepare a speech to persuade them.

Here's a sample: "I'm going to hand you forms to fill out. I want you to swear to me you're going to tell the truth. Don't be too positive, and don't be too negative. And the only person to judge the truth about your opinion is you. Can you promise to me to be a helpful and supportive coach to this other person (your boss), and not a cynic, critic, or judge? Because if he (she) tries to get better and all he hears back from you is cynicism or criticism, he gives up!"

Now put the same thing in language that you feel comfortable using.

As coach, you have to follow up with two groups:
1. The coached person
2. The stakeholders

You have to tell the coached person to ask for feedforward each month.

Now try writing in the space below the expression the coached person should use to ask for feedforward. Here is a model: "Based on my behavior last month, what ideas do you have for me next month?" Another phrase would be, "How can I be better in the future?" Or, "You know that I'm working at delegating more effectively. Over the past month, have you noticed a difference?"

The other part of a coach's job in following up is to make sure that a mini-survey is carried out. It can be as simple as one question with scoring from -3 to +3. Here is a model for the kind of question to ask:

"In the past X months, has this person become more effective or less effective as a listener?"

Now write your own version in the space below using the behavior YOU want to coach in a co-worker.

SECRETS OF A LEADERSHIP COACH 4 DEVELOPING A TEAM

Team building can be built on the principles of feedforward.

Before you get started on developing a team, you have to decide whether you really have a team. Many groups get confused about this, because they're really not a team. So the first question to ask a group of people is:

"Do you need to work together as a team, yes or no? Or is it that you just work together, and you're interdependent… but not a really a team working toward a common goal?"

In the space below, specifically address the issues of (1) need and (2) common goal to define your sample team for these exercises. Pick a real team you are involved in. If you aren't sure, pick a non-work group, like a sports group or your family. A typical response could be, "My marketing group is a team because we need to coordinate our different projects with different media advertising to convey the same message and because we have a common goal to sell X product."

Here's your next step: Survey the team with two questions to determine the gap between current team performance and how the team needs to perform. Here are the questions: "On a scale of 1 to 10, how well are you working together as a team now?" Everybody puts their individual score on a piece of paper, you collect them, divide them by the number of people in the group and you come up with a team score.

Then you ask the group a second question: "How well do we need to work together as a team?" (On a scale of 1 to 10).

For the sake of these exercises, enter your own answers to both questions in the space below.

Now that you have identified your gap, you need to figure out how to close the gap. The team should figure out two behaviors that everyone needs to work on to improve team behavior.

Write the two behaviors you believe your team needs to work on in the space below.

Write a good example of a question to get YOUR team started on helping each other using feedforward. Here is an excellent example: "How can I better help our team in the future?"

Now everyone uses feedforward to gather suggestions and come up with an area for his own area of improvement that fits into team goals.

Then one asks each month (or other interval) for feedforward on the area relevant to him. Let us say that your job is public relations and you are part of a product launch team. You might say this to your colleagues:

"My own area for behavioral improvement is communicating the goals of our organization.

"Based on my behavior last month, if you had an idea to help me this month, what would it be?"

Now you write down what your statement would be for your job in the team you picked.

We hope you enjoyed assembling your personal action plan in this way. It will give you a practical "take away" from the work you put into completing this series of courses.